Love Yourself, *Love Your Life!*

The Self-Love Handbook

Raechel "Dr. Rae" Rivers

Love Yourself,
Love Your Life!
The Self-Love Handbook

Embrace Enterprises & Publishing
www.raechelrivers.com
Cover Photo: Lance Thurman

Disclaimer and Terms of Use: The author and publisher has used her best efforts in preparing *Love Yourself, Love Your Life! The Self-Love Handbook.* She makes no warranties or representations with respect to the accuracy or completeness of the contents of this book and specifically disclaims any implied warranties of reader ability for a particular purpose. It is further acknowledged that the Author and Publisher assumes no responsibility for errors, omissions, or contrary interpretation of the subject matter herein. In practical advice books, like anything else in life, there are no guarantees of results. Readers are cautioned to reply on their own judgment about their individual circumstances and to act accordingly. This book is not intended for use as a source of mental, medical, health, or nutrition advice. All readers are advised to seek the services of competent mental, medical, health, and nutrition professionals.

Dedication
For My Family

Greetings,

My name is Raechel Rivers, but you can call me Dr. Rae! I am your Self-Love Advocate. These life lessons on love have prepared me for this position. I have always enjoyed writing and acting as sort of a therapist amongst friends; so Love Coaching it is. To get started down this path, I've created the *Self-Love Handbook* as a follow-up to my book, *Journey to Self: Journey to Love*. It was created with the intentional message of finding your life's purpose and focusing on it during the single season of your life. Your life is worth more than being in a relationship and finding your true love. I know from experience; and I wasted plenty of time in pursuit of relationships. Through it all, I lost myself. Through my journey, I had to find myself and become at peace with self and God who is within.

Maybe you are not single, but somehow *Love Yourself, Love Your Life! The Self-Love Handbook* has found you. I know many people who are married or in long-term relationships who are not happy or feel that something is still missing from their lives. I believe that the missing aspect is purpose. You may have an idea of what God, your Creator has called you to do; but you haven't figured it out yet. I am here to help you do just that; to discover or remember what it is that you love to do. Whether you are married to the love of your life or not, just know that God has created you to live a purpose-driven and meaningful life.

While participating in this program, reading the material, and going through the exercises, I want you to meditate on your ideal life and relationships. There will be many questions to answer regarding the current state of how you feel about yourself, your life, and your relationships. You will work through some of the tough questions which may be holding you back from living your ideal life. You were designed to heal yourself. You are resilient. No matter what has happened in your past or past relationships, you can heal; spiritually, mentally, emotionally, physically, and financially too. In fact, once you start living your purpose, you may find something that will create an opportunity for you to earn money and make a living doing what you love. Your healing begins within you. Make a decision today that you are going to love yourself and your life despite its current conditions. Good fortune can and will fall into your lap as you focus on loving yourself and living your purpose daily; creating happiness and keeping a positive mindset.

As you believe and continue to work on yourself and apply the thoughts and actions toward your ideal life, you will succeed. You will do some goal-setting and look at what it takes to achieve desired results. The ideal is that once you finish reading this book or participating in one of my workshops or one-on-one love coaching sessions, you will be on your way to creating the life that you desire and becoming a better you. You will learn to love yourself better today and always because it's a life-long journey. You don't need anyone to tell you to love yourself, but sometimes you need a reminder.

How do we truly love ourselves? Do we really know how? Some people portray that they do, but their actions do not always line up. We are all forever works in progress; and I feel as though we all need to take some time off to really assess our personal love walk; love of self, love of God, and love of others. This book is a simple guide on making that assessment and taking an inventory of your personal life. It is geared toward single people; but this book is also for those in love relationships or marriages. No matter what type of relationship in which you are involved, the interactions will always be a reflection of what's going on inside of you. The goal is to maintain a harmonious relationship with yourself, with God and your environment, and with others.

Thanks for participating, and I look forward to working with you personally!

Namaste and Love,

Dr. Rae

Self-Love Toolkit

Items you will need for your personal, self-paced, self-love healing process include:

-a pen or pencil

-a journal or notebook paper

-some quiet time away from distractions, i.e. TV, Internet, friends, family, and/or work

-your favorite music (something soothing and relaxing)

-sea salt, bath salts, and/or bubble bath, bath oil, spiritual cleanse bath (olive oil, lemons, sea salt) lavender, rose, sage, and/or patchouli oil.

-incense and/or scented candles

-blender

-food processor

Table of Contents

Love Yourself, *Love Your Life!*

Love Yourself, Love Your Life
Love Yourself and God

Relationships can be difficult; but let's talk about the one with self. How do you love yourself? Well, that's a peculiar question. It's all about how you treat yourself; how you feel about yourself; and how you conduct yourself in your relationships with others. Have you been neglecting the most important relationships in your life; the one with self and the one with God? You and God should be your top priority. I think sometimes we can focus so much on our need to please others that we forget about what's really important in life, including self and God. When you are unbalanced within, unhappy with self, and unhappy with life it is impossible to have healthy relationships with others. You will always seek an outside source for happiness, which does not equate real happiness. Happiness is within; it can be expressed through emotions. It is a state of mind that should be developed and unaltered by life conditions and circumstances. I'm not saying that we don't sometimes have bad days, but we must learn to possess an intrinsic motivation for what makes us happy. What is our reason for living? What is our purpose in life? A relationship alone is not going to fulfill this ultimate desire for happiness and purpose in life. We must learn and find out what we want from life and be happy with ourselves before getting into relationships. Otherwise, the relationships will lack balance. As it is within, so it will be without. Work on you; love God; love yourself; and love your life so that you can learn to better love others in a healthy way.

Scripture says it best that God is love in 1 John 4:8. "Whoever does not love does not know God, because God is love" (NIV). How can we say that we love God if we do not love our neighbor as we love ourselves? Better yet, how can we love our neighbor if we are not in right relationship with ourselves or God? God lives and dwells within us. When we have a relationship with God, then the world will see the fruit of that relationship; the fruit of His spirit and love that lives in you. It is time to heal that relationship within you. God's love is enough to sustain you until you learn to truly love yourself and your life despite your conditions!

Love Yourself, Love Your Life

You deserve to love your life! I know so many people who hate their lives. In fact, I have felt this way about my own life a time or two. The truth is, whatever you dislike about your life, you must change. That's what I've had to do and that's what I believe. "Life is too short to be unhappy so cheer up and live it"! This has been one of my mantras for several years now. I believe I began using it during graduate school when I found myself struggling with depression at times. What causes us to hate our lives? There are many factors that can contribute to feeling as if you hate your life. Not living out your life's purpose; an unfulfilling job; a bad relationship; not having enough money; being single or feeling alone; not using your gifts and talents. These are all factors that can be changed, believe it or not! You have the power within to change your life, but first you must heal from past relationships, hurts, and misfortunes in life by learning to better love yourself despite what has happened.

The key to loving your life is loving yourself. Loving yourself is the beginning of it all. We would say that it begins with loving God, but if we believe that God is in us, then loving yourself is the beginning of it all. I have heard many great teachers say this including the late Dr. Wayne Dyer and Essence Best Selling Author Tiphani Montgomery. In order to find your purpose and be happy in life, you must begin by loving yourself and nurturing the relationship you have with yourself and essentially God; a Higher Power, who lives right inside of you. This is where it begins.

Love Yourself, Love Your Life
Create the Life You Desire

Making changes, manifesting, and creating the life you desire is a process. You have to look within yourself. You have to first identify what you don't like; that is usually easy and apparent. What you complain about the most is what you would like to see change the most in your life (or relationships). This is where the negativity and complaint zone comes from because you "hate" these things; you "hate" your life, but what you focus on expands. "I hate_____." When you hate something you are really acknowledging what you want to see change in your life; and there is nothing wrong with wanting more or something better or different for your life. The truth is you NEVER have to stay "stuck" in anything you don't like—anything that goes against your heart's desires. In fact, that is sin (that is of the Devil). The Universe/God (Infinite Intelligence) is expansive. God gives us free will (Heaven). God gives us options. God is limitless! When you begin to understand this, everything you ask for (desire) will be yours. When one door closes, God has ten other doors that can be opened for you! The key is finding them; no, the key is knowing what you want…

You can work or take any job; but it may not be right for you if it doesn't line up with your life's purpose despite pay. Sometimes you may have to take a pay cut to be happy to live a meaningful life and work a meaningful job that makes you happy. You don't have to settle for a job that doesn't fit you. You don't have to settle for a job or working for someone at all so discover your life's purpose first. Many times people just take the first job offered because income is needed. This is called "drifting". If you do this, you may wind up hating the job and your life. Furthermore, when you drift into a job you may settle in pay. What's the point of working if you can't get ahead?

You have to feed your mind positivity after your purpose and what you hate have been identified. It's time to focus on making the changes to love yourself and your life. When you love yourself, you don't settle in unhappiness. You become what you think about. What you think about you bring about. Are we clear on this?

Now list the things you hate or would like to change about your life:

1.

2.

3.

4.

5.

Did you write out what you hate or what you would like to change? The first step to change is to recognize what needs to be changed. Now that you've identified what you "hate", let's identify what you love and what you want; what you desire to see manifest in your life. These ideals will be the opposite of what you hate. What would help you love your life and yourself? For example: More income; your soulmate; better health; a better job using your gifts, talents, and abilities.

I love or I would like to manifest:

1.

2.

3.

4.

5.

Only focus on these and don't complain! Act as if you've already made these changes. How would you feel if you already had the aspects that you desire? What you desire when you pray; you have not because you ask not. God knows what you need before you ask. Matthew 7:7 "knock and the door will open". Anything you ask in my name I'll do. With God all things are possible. These are all biblical sayings. ONLY focus on what you want! This or something better Lord! Your Creator knows you best; better than yourself. As you meditate on these things, you are bringing them into your existence with faith in God and yourself. Pray, have faith and gratitude; stay positive; exercise to release tension; go on nature walks; go outside; spend time with family or children; Have fun! Play, dance, sing, and celebrate! Get excited! Take action everyday on your new happy life! Visualize and feel your happiness every day!

Thank God in advance! Create a vision board. Release the old and surround yourself with other positive people if you can. You are in the process of creating your ideal life. It all happens from the inside out. You are victorious. You deserve to love your life! Listen to

Pharell's "Happy" song 20 times a day if you have to and get happy about your life. Life is a game. It starts in your mind. Go for it against all odds. God is supporting you; now follow your bliss! Volunteer; give back! Get your mind off of yourself and off of what you hate.

Love Yourself, Love Your Life
Life Purpose
(Exercise 1)

Have you discovered your life's purpose?

My life's purpose is _____.

I believe God created me to _____.

If you are unsure, make a list of what you love to do.

I love to or I enjoy:

1.
2.
3.
4.
5.

What are you good at doing?

1.
2.
3.
4.
5.

God has given us many gifts and talents; and our life's purpose allows us to use them on the job, at home, at church, and just about anywhere in any setting. How do you get a job or create an income around your purpose? After you identify what you love, enjoy, or a cause you want to fight for, now look for a job where you can get paid to do what you love! You can also start a business or project and create an income doing what you love. Once you start living out your purpose, you will begin to love your life. You will feel like a kid again; you will be serving others and making money, or not. Your purpose is something that you enjoy or would do for free!

When you are not living a purpose-driven life, you will feel unfulfilled and as though you are settling. I don't believe in settling at all! I've settled in relationships and jobs; and in doing so, I lost my way trying to please everyone but myself. Afraid of what others might think of me. Just taking any job or staying in relationships that were damaging instead of benefiting me.

Since moving back to St. Louis, MO, my hometown, four years ago, I have quit every job I ever had. Why, you ask? Because although they provided me with income, which wasn't enough to live off of sufficiently, they were jobs unrelated to what I spent twelve years of college studying. The jobs were unsatisfying with low wages. I couldn't understand why I was unable to land a professional position in my field that paid me enough money to make a decent living. Looking back on the last four years, I now understand that my purpose was to use my frustration with the jobs and create my own businesses which I've done. I've learned that I will never be satisfied working any traditional job. This may not be your path. You may love your job, but for me, being an Entrepreneur is my destiny.

Love Yourself, Love Your Life
What Is Your I Am?

First of all, who is I am? God tells us in the Old Testament, in the Bible, I am that I am. Do you know how much power is in that statement I am? Jesus said the same thing. "Who do they say I am"? We cannot separate ourselves from God, from Christ, the Son of God. If God is our Father and Jesus is our brother, and they live in us and they left us with the Holy Spirit, then why can't we *"I am"* something? Did you know that you can *I am* something? The word "am" is an action verb used to describe. I know that even when learning about verbs in English "am" is a difficult one to define. What is am? Am means "to be" so "am" must always possess something. Whatever it attaches itself to, that's what it is. So be mindful when you "am" something because there is so much power in what you are saying or "am"ing (bringing into being); positive or negative. It's easy to "am" whatever your emotions tell you to am. For example, when you feel tired or beat down, what do you say? *I am tired* or if you feel sad or depressed, *I am depressed*. These negative affirmations based on how you feel send signals to your mind or mental state and essentially out into the Universe. What you send out in word, thought, deed, or action you attract to yourself.

Why do I feel it necessary to break this down for you? I want you to become aware of your feelings and mindset and how it affects your actions which create your life. You are always attracting things to yourself and the power of life and death is in your tongue. Even in Romans, Paul said to call things that be not (are not). You must have the faith of Father Abraham when choosing to love yourself and your life. It really is a mind game. Life is a game. You are always choosing. No matter what has happened to you in the past, including yesterday, you must have the faith that you can change your life and be happy with God's help. You can outwit the tricks of the devil your enemy who is sometimes within (we are our own worst enemy). For every positive there is a negative; but don't get stuck in your belief of the negative. That is where the enemy will keep you; and that is where he can use you. At that point, God is not using you.

God wants you healthy, happy, whole and focused on every blessing little or big. When you are faithful in the little, that's when He can make you a ruler over much. God is the Source of all that you will ever need; and just like earthly fathers who give gifts so does your heavenly father if you believe Him. He can right now, pour out an abundance of rain and blessings, however it has to be in His timing. He has to know that you are faithful. He just wants to be loved and glorified. The answer to your every prayer and need is already within you; because He is within you. Begin today to thank Him and praise Him for everything because your gratitude is what increases your latitude. When you get excited about life, when you are happy, when you are positive, you attract more and more opportunities and blessings and positive life experiences. On the other hand, when you are negative and focused on all that's bad, guess what happens? You attract more of that. What is your I am again I ask? We will deal more with this topic in another section where I provide personal examples of I am affirmations, and you will create your own at that time.

Love Yourself, Love Your Life
Life Purpose

Your Life's Purpose is always with you and will always be with you. It is what you think about before you go to sleep, and first on your mind when you wake up in the morning. To many it may sound like I'm describing the feeling you have for a special person. Love of your Life's Purpose is that same feeling; the feeling you have for your Soulmate or someone who you believe is your Soulmate. Why is finding and having a Life Purpose so important? Your "definiteness of purpose" as Napoleon Hill defined, gives you meaning and focus in life. Your purpose gives you something for which to live. Why do you get up every morning? Why are you living? Maybe you don't know. Maybe you have drifted away from what you really love. That will happen at times; sometimes we lose sight of purpose because life can be tough. Living this life is all about our perception of what happens to us not just what happens to us. It's okay if you haven't defined your exact purpose. It's not always one thing and can be several things. The most important aspect is that you choose something to focus on while you have time on this side of the Earth.

Your life's purpose is something you can pray and meditate on. In fact, you may find that it is something that has been with you and in you since childhood; because God placed it in you. You don't need to consult with anyone or need anyone's permission to do what you feel called to do. You will feel so much better about your life once you get in alignment with this special calling. You will be excited about life! You will not be persuaded to get down about what you can't control; even the people in your life who you surely can't control. You just embrace everything about you, and the tugging of the Spirit of God within that's telling you what to do. You want to be happy deep down inside, and only you know what really makes you happy. It doesn't matter where you live or what people come and go from your life. When you are in pursuit of your purpose, when you are living your purpose, nothing and no one can get in your way! You are focused on what you need to do. It may be a calling to help others in some way. Usually, it will involve some type of help or service for others although maybe not in the beginning. When you are fostering this purpose, it may seem as though you are being selfish because you have to take time out to prepare for it. Prepare yourself for the people you are called to help. You may be a researcher, a writer, a teacher, a police officer, doctor, or lawyer. Think of almost any occupation; think about entrepreneurs or people in business or ministry. Every calling involves a process of learning and training, but in the end, what you learn along with your gifts and talents will ultimately benefit someone else as well as yourself.

Begin to get a clear picture about what you really want to do. Only focus on that. Focus on what you want to happen in your life and what you want to have in your life; not on what you don't want to happen or what you don't have. You have to trick your brain and begin to "act as if"…act as if you already possess everything that you DESIRE. Trust God and the Universe to help you make it happen. "Don't worry, be happy" because your life can change in an instant! Everyday affirm your purpose; and everyday look for new opportunities to pursue it! Know that ABUNDANCE is more than money. Abundance is peace, love, happiness, joy, family, and friends. Meditate on all that is good in your life and more goodness will be added unto you! It's your life to live so start living it with a DEFINITE PURPOSE and FAITH!

Love Yourself, Love Your Life
Life Purpose

"What do you want to be when you grow up?" My Professor at Langston University, Dr. Alex Lewis, would ask me that all the time. He knew then back in 2004 that I still hadn't grasped who I wanted to become. I was drifting through life trying to figure it out like most people do. I was twenty-one years old. For three years I worked at Langston University, my Alma Mater, an HBCU (Historically Black College and University) while pursuing my Masters degree in Urban Education. Life in Langston, Oklahoma involved some of the best and worst times, but it was a great place to be at that time for me to grow, develop, and learn. It was a comfort zone; a safe place to realize your dreams. I developed so many friendships and received guidance from so many Mentors who saw greatness in me when I tried to hide and blend in with everyone else. They saw so many talents within me that they nurtured me all the way to pursue a Doctoral program at the University of Arkansas in Fayetteville, AR.

With all this guidance, I had still missed the mark. I didn't conduct any exercises such as the ones in this book.

I wish at 18, 21, or at 25 I would have used a program such as this *Self-Love Handbook* to discover my true calling. This is why I am here to create it now…to help others young and old because it's never too late to do what God has called you to do. However, if I would have conducted a self-assessment early on in my young adult life, I may have achieved my dreams and purpose faster. I'd be rich and famous by now. I do not regret any of the lessons I've learned along the way. In case you're wondering, during my Junior year of college, which is normally when you choose your major; my decision was between Broadcast Journalism and Business. I chose to pursue a business degree. I didn't realize that I could have chosen to study both fields. Looking back, my best grades and highest interests were always in my English courses. I loved writing even then. I didn't know that I would love teaching until now, but just as the scripture says all things work together for good. People have often told me that even my name sounds like a famous person or a news reporter. I'm living proof that you can be whomever you chose or decide to be. Don't limit God or yourself! These days, my generation changes careers several times. We are the generation to "create our own thing"; we are not afraid to step outside the box. You can't be or you will miss the mark of what God is doing. If you don't act on the ideas he has given you, someone else will. Long gone are the days of feeling limited and locked into one job or profession. Welcome to the age of "Multiple Streams of Income". This life is not for everyone, but everyone who is brave and passionate enough to pursue every desire within their heart. Brave enough to create their desired life.

In choosing to pursue a Business degree, I was right on target. Even as a little girl, I was always making and selling things; quite the entrepreneurial-minded kid. I had no idea that 30 years later God would allow me to use all my gifts and talents for my own businesses. Even in my high school Senior book, I remember stating that I wanted to own several businesses; we become what we think, write, and act. "We have many gifts and talents and we don't know which ones will be called upon", my friend Anise told me. We work for God.

Love Yourself, Love Your Life
Life Purpose
(Exercise 2)

What Do You Want To Be When You Grow Up?

<u>Part 1</u>

Take a few minutes to remember what you wanted to be as a child. How does that line up with your life today? Did you become that person or pursue that career path? Why or why not? If you don't remember what you wanted to be, what do you remember doing or playing as a child?

<u>Part 2</u>

The questions below are for self-study and reflection as you discover or remain on course with your life's purpose.

1) Are you living a purpose-driven life? What does that look and feel like for you?

2) Are you happy with your life? Do you feel fulfilled?

3) What do you believe is your God-given purpose? What has God shown you or lead you to or placed within your heart to do?

4) What are you good at doing? What are your gifts and talents?

5) What do you love to do? What brings you joy? What are you passionate about?

6) How are you serving? (Community, Church, Family, Workplace)

7) Are you striving to be like Christ? How do you represent Christ in your daily life?

Think about your high school or college life experience. In what activities did you participate? What were your interests? Are you still nurturing those activities and interests? Think about how those can lead you to your purpose-driven life. What courses did you take pleasure in or excel in? In what ways did you or do you serve or volunteer at school, home, church, or in your community?

Self-Love

Self-Love
Healing (Loving) from Within

It's about balance…As it is within (internally), so it will be without (externally)…everything from our home environment; to how we conduct our jobs (or the type of job we have); to our relationships with others is a reflection of what's going on inside of us. We have to be right or feel good within and about ourselves in order to manifest harmonious relationships with others; including those with family, friends, co-workers, and intimate love relationships. We are in a constant state of expelling energy by our mere presence. Our mental, emotional, and spiritual state will emanate from us positive or negative energy. The state of our inner being, healthy or not, will have an effect on our relationship with our environment and those with whom we interact…Like attracts like…We want to be in a constant state of attracting positive life and love experiences, but it begins within…

How do I love myself?
I eat right…I live right…
I'm good to myself and my body…
I create my own happiness…I am love…

What is Self-Love?

Knowing yourself and accepting yourself is the beginning of loving yourself. "Learning to love yourself is the greatest love of all". You can't truly love someone else until you fully learn to love yourself. These all sound so cliché, but they are all so true. What is self-love and why is this topic so important? Self-love is age-less, race-less, class-less, gender-less, and without sexual orientation. Do you love yourself? Yes! You do! Do you need someone to tell you how to love yourself or that you need to love yourself? Sometimes we need gentle reminders that the Universe/God is going to give you anyway when you are out of alignment or not practicing self-love.

Self-love is a holistic love of self; not egotistically or out of ego in vanity. To practice self-love is to love one's self. Self-love is a day-to-day, ongoing process that will challenge and surprise us throughout our lifetime. Everyone loves his or herself; we are selfish by nature. When we are born as little babies, it's all about "me, me, me". We then learn how to share and get along with family and others. As we grow and learn, the way we interact with people stems from learned behaviors. Sometimes in our growing, learning, and sharing process, we become unbalanced. It begins in childhood as we start coming into our own person and personality and trying to find groups, sometimes family sometimes not, in which to fit. We begin to navigate toward sameness or like-mindedness; those who share our commonalities even at an early age. Sometimes we may discover that we just don't fit.

So where did we first lose confidence or love for ourselves? When someone told us we were different or teased us for being different. If we didn't know to embrace being different then, we were offended and hurt and maybe even sensitive about it. We cried about it as kids and tried to find ways to alter it or mask it as adolescents. Some of us have carried these ways into adulthood constantly seeking acceptance and approval from others; trying to fit-in, but not. Pretending to be happy but neglecting who the person inside really is.

Now is the time to heal that child inside so that you can move into a life of purpose and real happiness. Real love of yourself; accepting everything about you, good, bad, and ugly (there is no ugly). It doesn't matter where you start from, at some point you have to accept yourself.

If you find things you don't like, you change them. Your goal is your happiness. When you love and accept you, not in vanity but in a healthy and balanced way, you have more of you and love to give others whether they accept you or not. They don't have to accept you, but they will respect you because you shine.

Loving yourself and knowing yourself prepares you for relationships with others. You may be longing for partnership; you may feel misunderstood; you may have had bad break-ups or divorce; you may have issues with family members, friends, and co-workers; you may feel everyone around you is crazy; you may feel like a doormat and as if everyone takes advantage of you. These characteristics mean you are out of balance. You can say you love yourself, but you're not acting like you do. Self-love involves learning to put yourself and your needs before others. There is nothing selfish about this. Your environment is a reflection of you. Your peace, love, and balance come from within then radiate out. When you take care of you first, you feel better. You are in a better and healthier position to help others or be there for your loved ones. Put your oxygen mask on first (save you), and then save who you can. If you are dying or lost, how can you help someone else? How can you learn to love yourself better or stay in balance? Learning about you and to love yourself and studying yourself is a life-long process. It should be fun. It teaches you what you like and don't like; and what you will and won't tolerate in your life.

Dr. Rae's Hierarchy of Self-Love & Self-Actualization (5 Self-Love Needs)

1. Mind

2. Body

3. Heart

4. Spirit

5. Emotions

Self-Love Assessment

1. Mind- What are you thinking? How are you thinking? Positively or negatively? Is the glass half full or half empty?

2. Body- What are you eating? & Why? What is the source of your attachment to certain foods? (ex: comfort foods, sugar, ice cream, alcoholic beverages, coffee) Is there an emotional attachment to your food? What is the culture of the social environment in which you eat? Do you participate in some form of regular exercise?

3. Heart- What are you holding onto toward people in your past? Bitterness? Anger? Is your heart hard, sad, or angry about past relationship situations? (This is related to emotions as well).

4. Spirit- How is your spiritual life? Your faith practices or faith level? Your belief system? (This is related to mind).

5. Emotions- What state do you find yourself in emotionally on most days? How do you feel when you wake up in the morning? (This is related to holding things in your heart).

Note:

If any of the 5 Self-Love Needs are not in alignment, it will be difficult to reach any goals; love goals, personal goals, or even daily goals with the desired permanent changes.

Self-Actualization and Healing

Self-love begins with and is in the mind, body, heart, spirit, and emotions. *The Self-Love Handbook* uses a holistic approach to a better you. It is a path to personal freedom; being able to love yourself while achieving your personal and love goals. There is nothing wrong with desiring a Mate, but first you must prepare yourself for him or her. You must be in an overall healthy state in order to attract the healthy relationship(s) you desire and deserve; not only with the opposite sex, but with family, spouses, children, friends, and even in the workplace. As you become conscious of your mental, physical, spiritual, and emotional state of being, you also become aware of how being in an unhealthy state affects your relationships. You will realize that as you self-actualize (become the best inner you) that your outer world has no choice but to come into alignment with a healthy more balanced and desirable you.

You must learn to let go of the old you to embrace and achieve the new you. People who truly love themselves want for and lack for nothing for they know well the true Source of love, God. God is love, and God provides. Self-love is not selfish. It will resemble characteristics of selflessness at times. It also seeks nothing in return; it emulates that "love is patient, love is kind. It does not envy, it does not boast, it is not proud. It is not rude, it is not self-seeking, it is not easily angered, it keeps no record of wrongs. Love does not delight in evil but rejoices with the truth. It always protects, always trusts, always hopes, always perseveres. Love never fails" (1 Corinthians 13:4-8, NIV).

Once this state is achieved in mind, it will expect this perception of love in every relationship; it gives off vibrations of this type of love. Therefore, it receives this love.

Realizing Your Self-Love Goals

Self-love healing begins by assessing where you are when it comes to loving yourself, and where you would like to be. Take some time to figure out your purpose for utilizing this program. Remember you attract that which you are. How can you work on yourself in order to have harmonious relationships with others? This program is all about you. You can choose to allow others to dictate how you will act, or you can take control by consciously deciding how you will react to others. The only person you can control is yourself. You can make a conscious effort to love yourself despite the actions, non-actions, or reactions of others. When you are truly happy within, you give off a vibration that alerts others of who you are and how much you love yourself. You have to love yourself enough not to settle for the mistreatment or disrespect of others.

Use the following questions on the next few pages to begin realizing your self-love goals. Write your answers in your journal or in the spaces provided.

1. What are your self-love goals?

2. How do you plan to achieve these goals?

3. How do you view your environment or the people in your environment?

4. What is your role in the relationships that you would like to focus on?

5. How can you make sure that your needs are met despite the demands of others? (This includes demands from family, friends, and/or co-workers; any relationship that you can think of.)

Realizing Your Self-Love Goals
(Worksheet)

1) What do you seek from this program?

2) What are your personal goals?

3) What is your current reality/perception of yourself?

4) If it is negative, how will you begin to change it?

5) What steps will you take to better love yourself?

6) Do you have a pampering or a "me" time regimen? ie. (getting your hair and nails done; massage; alone time to do what you want; see a movie; read a book; go shopping; enjoy a meal; pray/meditate; non-work; play; go to the gym; cleaning your home- a clean home is a reflection of your mind).

7) How often do you practice it?

8) What is your personal definition of self-love?

9) What do you desire for yourself and your life overall?

Dealing With Your Past
The Art of Letting Go
(Worksheet)

1) What would you change about your past?

2) What have you learned from your past or past relationships?

3) What is the best way for you to be able to let go and move on?

4) What personal goals can you work on to re-focus your energy from past disappointments?

Forgiveness

Forgive yourself and those who hurt you from childhood to teenage years, adulthood, and your parents or even other adults. Let go, let God; be healed and receive it. Release past hurts from your heart. Don't walk around with years of pain. You will not be able to advance or truly fully be happy if you don't forgive. True healing begins when you are able to release past hurts from your heart. Who do you need to forgive?

List the names: (including yourself)

1.

2.

3.

4.

5.

6.

7.

Prepare For Your Soulmate(s)

We have many Soulmates but only one Twin Flame, who may be too much like us (you); so pray for your "compatible" Soulmate. May God bring to you and reveal to you your compatible Soulmate. Who you are looking for is looking for you. Soulmates help you along your life's journey. There are always lessons to learn in life. Soulmates are good for you, but they can also be bad for you; or tough relationships that you've encountered. Ultimately, they help you learn life lessons.

On a Soul level, you have chosen your life path, life experiences, and Soulmates. Your Soulmate has most likely been with you before in another lifetime. Pray that God will line you up in this lifetime with your compatible Soulmate. Soulmates are not always related to the opposite sex; and they can also be people who are different races, ages, and religions from you. We have family and friends who have travelled with us before too; they are called our Soul Family Mates. You know that feeling you get when you first meet someone, and you feel like you have known them before or forever? That's because you have; your Soul recognizes them.

Life is all about learning lessons and purpose; God's purpose. Same sex partners have Soulmates too. Within your Soul is where your male or female energy resides; which you may have manifested in a physical form (male) (female) differently. These life lessons prepare us for the next.

Law of Attraction: Use It

Are you using the Law of Attraction in your life? Whether you are conscious of it or not, you are in fact using this powerful law daily and throughout your day. You don't believe me? Well I've seen it work in my life for years, even when I didn't know what it was called. With the law of attraction, we use the concept of faith, intention, meditation, and visualization; all wrapped in one powerful package which is ultimately the power of your mind and focus. What is it that you truly desire for your life? You can attract the life or love that you so desire by the power of your thoughts and emotions. With the use of this law, you create the life of your deepest deserving and most loving desires.

Self-Love
(Exercise 1)

It is time to go within…

Reach deeply inside of yourself and dig…dig up old
hurts…dig up the past…breathe in…dig…breathe
out…release it!

Doesn't that feel good…do this at least 10
times…slowly…breathe in as you dig…and breathe
out…to release…

Now let's do some journaling… (write these questions in
the spaces provided below or in your Self-Love
journal/notebook).

How can I really release the past?

What can I do differently in the future to protect myself in
relationships with others?

How do I see myself?
(Likes/Dislikes)

What can I do to better love myself?

How can I put myself first and make sure my needs are met?

What do I want from a relationship that I can't give myself?

Do I want from a relationship or am I willing to give to a relationship?

Am I healthy, whole, and complete without a relationship?

What are my highest ideals and aspirations for myself?

How can I begin to work toward my greatest ideals of myself?

How to Love Yourself Better
Things to Do

1) Work on Your Appearance:

When you look good, you feel good. Working on your appearance may include getting new clothes, shoes, a new hairstyle, exercising, and eating right. Your appearance is outer; and when you accept how you look, you shine bright. You will have an inner-glow and designer labels, hair length, or even your dress size will not matter. How do you feel about yourself when you look in the mirror? It's not about what others think or feel about you. How do you feel? If you don't like what you see, change it and work on it, but be your authentic self.

2) Work on Your Health:

Your health is holistic. It is mental, physical, spiritual, and emotional; multifaceted. Do you feel healthy in these areas? You may need doctors or the guidance of holistic experts to help you regain balance, mentally, physically, spiritually, and emotionally. These aspects are all connected. When one part is unbalanced, it affects your whole body. You may need to consult a physician, personal trainer, nutritionist, or mental health professional to help assess any problem areas to make sure you are in optimal health. A part of loving yourself is taking care of your body when something doesn't feel right in any of those areas.

3) Assess Your Relationships and Your Role in Them:
Ask yourself what you will tolerate from others and from yourself. Are you giving too much? Seek out like-minded individuals and find groups who like to do what you do.

4) Spend Time Alone:
When you spend time alone, you have the opportunity to learn and study yourself. Ask yourself do you act like you love yourself? What are you eating? (Which affects your body) How are you in relationships? Do you go with the flow or step out on your own? Do you compromise to try to fit in with others? What do you like or like to do?

5) Celebrate Yourself:

What are your gifts and talents? Are you using them? Learn to love you. People can't help but love you when you love you!

6) Give Back:

Once you align with you, you are in a position to share your love with others and the world. Love you first, treat yourself right then you can't help but treat others right including family, friends, and strangers. Share your new found love of you with others and with the world; church, non-profits; organizations. Engage in community service. It's not just about you; and you are not seeking approval from others because you approve of yourself!

How I Did It!

In May of 2010, I made a personal life-changing commitment to my health. I had been in graduate school, pursuing a PhD for four years, and I'd accumulated so much weight while seeking to attain this endeavor. I was almost 200 pounds, not my natural weight, the year before I decided to make a change. I was happy, but not completely happy with what the scale read. That scale was liar! Although finding clothing was not an issue, I realized that I'd soon be turning 30 in four months, and I wanted to personally challenge myself. I had tried everything from juice fasting, to working out at the gym, to the Beyoncé lemonade diet, and even the Mayo Clinic diet; but nothing was exciting or held my attention long enough for me to be consistent. I needed a diet and lifestyle change which included raw food and light exercise; walking and meditating at the park. There are no quick fixes, but this worked fast for me. I lost approximately 11lbs in about 21 days and overall about 35lbs in one year due to a vegetarian diet. It takes three weeks to break bad habits and that's what I did.

I wanted to break the myths about aging so I made a commitment to myself through my diet. I had fun creating my own recipes, committed myself to my new diet, and never looked back. I currently maintain my weight through my new diet-style and habits that I developed because I personally never want to see the scale hit 200lbs again unless I'm carrying my first born. It's all up to you. You decide what you want for you and your look. What look or weight or size makes you feel at your best? Fall in love with you! The overall goal is to be healthy; you can be skinny and unhealthy so be careful not to remove too many certain healthy foods from your diet. It is best to consult a nutritionist for your overall weight loss and fitness goals.

Self-Love Detox

One of the major ways in which you can better love yourself is to monitor what type of substances you put into your body including; drugs, alcohol, and food. The Self-Love Detox is a 5 to 7 day fast created to assist you with your self-love goals. Some participants may choose to better love themselves and create a new body image by weight loss. Others may view this as a spiritual cleanse and a need to realize any co-dependencies on food, drugs, or alcohol. The body was designed to heal itself, and in order to gain clarity and really see yourself; and realize your self-love and relationship goals, you must begin by detoxifying and purifying your body. This will in turn assist you in mind renewal; and true emotional and physical healing from past hurts can begin. You don't even realize how much dead weight or old issues you actually carry around in the body. Our "fat" is used as a protection from our environment. As you begin to release the past, you also detoxify and release unwanted and unhealthy weight.

Raw and uncooked foods, fruit, vegetables, and nuts, are considered higher vibration foods. They will make you feel lighter and have more energy. When food is cooked, including meat, vegetables, fruit, and dairy products, you often feel heavy after eating them. These lower vibration foods will make you want to be lethargic or just sleep. For the purpose of the self-love detox you will stick to eating raw and uncooked foods not meat or animal products.

You will start with the Self-Love Basic Green Smoothie. You will need 1 cup of frozen pineapples (or fresh), 1 cup of frozen strawberries (or fresh), about a cup and a half of uncooked spinach, about a cup or more of distilled, alkaline, or spring water, and one banana. Add more bananas for a sweeter taste. Blend these together in a blender until smooth. Use more or less water for appropriate thickness of your liking. You can drink this smoothie 3 times a day throughout your detox or as often as you like. You can drink it alone or with additional raw food items including salads, fruits, and nuts. You can also use any type of fruits or greens that you prefer for your smoothies. Part of self-love healing includes experimenting with different foods that are healthy for you; so that you can begin to form new habits that will have lasting effects once put into practice.

Self-Love
(Exercise 2)

1) Turn your cell phone off or to the silent mode

2) Turn on your favorite soothing music

3) Draw a warm to hot bath; put real sea salt in it. Sprinkle about ½ of a handful. Put in some olive oil and a squeezed lemon (optional) or your favorite scented oil from your self-love toolkit (without the lemon); this is your self-love healing, detoxification and relaxation bath; and you will feel so good once you re-emerge from the water.

4) Time to get in a nice soft spot like your bed, favorite chair or couch. If it's close to night time, I say sleep naked especially if you are single. There isn't a more liberating feeling than the comfort of your sheets especially if they are the really soft ones. If you aren't that brave, a silk or polyester gown will do; something to feel good up against your skin.

5) Boil some water for a good herbal tea or just drink some water (not cold) room temperature after that nice hot bath.

6) Time to do some journaling. Reflect on your day in your self-love Notebook from your toolkit. Think about your self-love goals. a) Think about the state of your current love-life. b) Think about your desired state of your love-life. Think about your relationship goals. Remember the most important one is the one with yourself and your Creator. This is your time to embrace the Spirit of God to help you better love yourself and to heal your heart, mind, and emotions.

Ask yourself: Am I trying too hard? Am I repelling love? What kind of energy vibration am I giving off? Is it loving or demanding of others? You can only control you. No matter how hard you try to manipulate others into loving you, let them love the way they love. Your job is to love you (meet your own needs) and to be loving.

7) Say a prayer; meditate then rest (nap) or go to bed. Releasing your prayer is the power of relaxing into self-love by replenishing your spirit. Now rest; tomorrow is another day!

Self-Love Prayer

Almighty Creator of the Universe and Creator of Me, Teach Me how to better love myself. Show Me that the state of my love-life is in your Divine Order. Help Me to learn how to be loving despite others actions, non-actions, and re-actions. Fill Me with your love today and always. Allow Me to radiate with love in all that I think, say, and do; for I AM LOVE just like you. –Amen

Affirmations

What Is Your I Am?
The Parable of the Sower

What are you believing God for in this Season of your life? Each one of us "Believers" are praying and requesting something of the Lord. If I told you the truth about what's really going on in my life right now, I don't know if you would believe me. I am currently in many situations that I need the Lord to help me with. Does that sound like you? I'm trying to figure out how I ended up here. I often question God; but God doesn't make mistakes. We do make mistakes in our effort to figure out life without allowing Him to lead the way. Not my will Father, but your will be done. What does that really look like? To be in a position of total surrender to your Creator? Even when we think we have life figured out the enemy, the devil, the hater of your Soul will come against you time and time again. But I'm reminded in James 1:1 that our trials are a testing of our faith. Isn't this what life is about? Having faith! What does that look like to you? Trusting God every step of the way. Trusting when He tells you to move or stay. Trusting the things that He tells you that may seem so strange and out of the ordinary.

One of the most fascinating things that I find about God is that He has given us a brain to think; hands to work; and a spirit to live to fulfill our call. He has placed His purposes within us; yet many of us continue to miss the mark when we don't pursue what God has given us through our gifts and talents. Just like in the Parable of the Sower. The master was not pleased with the servant who buried his talent. Each one of us has a special talent that God has placed inside of us. I was sitting in church on Sunday, November 16, 2014 and the Spirit was prompting me about this book which I had been saying that I would write for years. The 1st Edition was written in 2013. I used it in my first Self-Love Workshop, but I knew that I needed to add to the book. My mom, who was one of my staff members for the workshop said, "this book should be published". She was so correct; and "everyone who missed the workshop missed some really good information". Actually, the *Self-Love Handbook* was a grand idea I had around the same time my first book released in 2011. It was always set to be my second book. I just never knew how it would all come together. There were so many challenges that I had to face internally and externally in order for this project to finally come together. The time is NOW for this project! Your gifts will make room for you.

Affirmations
Prayers

Abundance

Abundance is within me- It surrounds me. I have all that I need and more. I am also filled with joy. I am full of love, which is God. Love surrounds me. There is no lack in my life. I am a cheerful giver. I also receive. I keep the cycle going. I am faithful. I am whole and complete. I am saved. God is my Source.

Written: September 10, 2009

Love

I AM Love. My presence is inconceivable. I am powerful. I am strong. I am holy. It is difficult to deny me. I am sacrifice. I am unconditional and eternal. The binds of hate are broken by my power. I do not lack because everything I need is within me. I am grace and beauty. I shine, I am love. I attract goodness and genuine people into my life.

Written: September 16, 2009

Inner Peace

I possess the peace that surpasses all understanding. I am peaceful and filled with joy and love. I have no worries. My hope and trust are in the Lord. He is my strength. He created me to solely depend on Him. His love and care overtakes me! I am at peace and my Soul is at rest.

Written: October 14, 2009

Patience

I am patient with myself and others. I am patient with my life and how its events are unfolding. Everything is in Divine Order. I do not give up on God's Plan for my Life. I am responsible for each decision and action I make to See His Plan Through. I am accountable. I am patient with me!

Written: January 20, 2010

Joy

Joy comes in the morning. I cry tears of joy, healing, and a refreshing. Joy comes from a deep place within. It sustains me even in tough times. I embrace joy in the morning!

Written: April 20, 2010

Discernment

I am able to discern what's best for my life. I hear God and I listen to my Higher Self. I recognize all that is good for my life. I let go of people and situations that do not mirror my Highest Good. I embrace my ability to know and everything is in Divine Order.

Written: June 13, 2010

Wisdom

Wisdom comes from God, the Creator and Source of All. I embrace Divine Knowledge. I apply good decision-making to my life, based on my experiences. Wisdom is my teacher. Wisdom guides my life.

Written: July 31, 2010

Affirmations

Write your own personal affirmations.

What is your I AM?

Call those things that be not… Romans 4:18

What would you like to manifest in your life? It could involve all of the previously mentioned affirmations, which are in the form of prayers, or it could be just one sentence. *Act as if you have already received…*

Example: I am rich! I am purposed! I am prosperous! I am LOVE therefore I attract love!

_____

_____

_____

_____

_____

_____

Self-Love
(Exercise 3)

Create a mental picture of the ideal you; one with realistic boundaries. See yourself achieving your dreams or desired state. How can you best bring these desires into manifestation? Do you believe you can?

What are you willing to sacrifice or give up for the new healthier you? TV; cigarettes; coffee; sex; meat; alcohol. It takes 21 days to break some habits, but a lifetime to implement a new lifestyle. Are you willing to change some things about your lifestyle to make your self-love goals permanent?

Use a daily journal to record your thoughts about moving from the old you to the new you. Release past hurts and relationships as well as the lessons learned through your writing. Write letters to the old you. Discuss the plans of the new, happier, healthier you.

Jot down your accomplishments and progress throughout the journey to self-love as well. Begin to affirm your self-love by using affirmations. Write your own self-love mission statement. Make promises to yourself.

Never look back! Keep moving forward to the abundant life and relationships that a complete, whole individual creates because of your healthy state. A good future is yours for the taking!

"Self-Love"

Everyday I'm finding me
And who I want to be
Everyday I'm becoming a better me
I accept me
And I love me for who I AM
I AM special, unique, and divine
I was created for a purpose

My past does not define me
I start from today
My future is bright
I love me and I love others
I only tolerate the best for my life
I am healthy and whole

I AM Love
I represent my Creator
I shine bright
I give myself to the world
And it is a better place because of me

Little Black Girl

Little Black Girl
Do you know you are beautiful?
Kinky Hair
And Dark Skin
Don't change You

Little Black Girl
Your skin has been kissed
By the Sun (Son)
You hold the world in your womb
Like Mother Africa

You have the power
To birth many nations
Did you know they all started with you?

Little Black Girl
You are a Goddess
Rubies, Diamonds, and Gold
They stole from you
Your crown is within now

Little Princess
Don't change You
There is so much of God in you
You are a healer too…

Thank You

You have been purposed to *Love Yourself, Love Your Life!* "We know that all things work for good for those who love God, who are called according to His purpose" (Romans 8:28, NAB). Trust in God, your Creator, not man. I believe in you…

Additional Resources

www.dherbs.com
By Djehuty Ma'at-Ra

Think & Grow Rich
By Napoleon Hill

Outwitting the Devil
By Napoleon Hill

The Game of Life and How to Play It
By Florence Scovel Shinn

The Bible
Various Versions: New American Bible (NAB), New
International Version (NIV), King James Version (KJV),
English Standard Version (ESV)

Made in the USA
Middletown, DE
31 January 2025

69991095R00057